# HOW TO HYPNOTIZE A LOBSTER

# HOW TO HYPNOTIZE A LOBSTER

## POEMS BY
## KRISTIN ROSE JUTRAS

*atmosphere press*

*For Brandon & Fee & Fred*

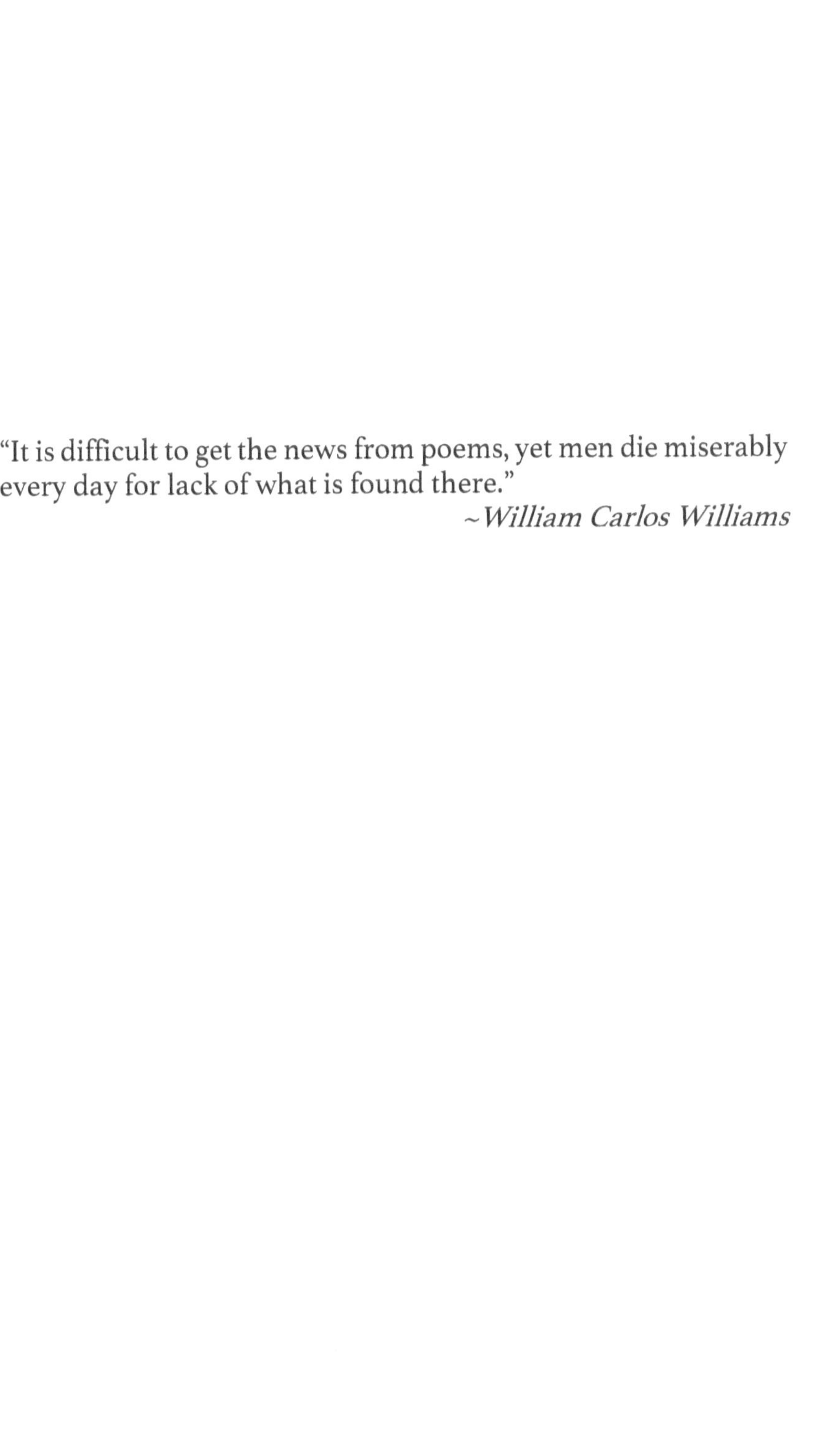

# CONTENTS

# PART I

"There's no vocabulary for love within a family, love that's lived in, but not looked at, love within the light of which all else is seen, the love within which all other love finds speech. This love is silent."

*~ T.S. Eliot*

## CROOKED POND

You told us never to go down
to the three bears' house alone – the snapping turtles guard it, you said.
My brother and I paddled that day, the red rowboat splintering and
creaking

                    the dark water

The trees sick with hemlock

    disease

          and I wondered
           if it had to do with that
man you talked about, what was his name?
Sophocles?

    Euripedes?      Merlin or

      Arthur?


    These names graveled bags of sea glass in my mouth


       The pond had flooded the bears' house
Leonard the frog


    and Maude the toad came along for
protection I wore my skirt sewn of laurel leaves,
      loosed my hair,
        mermaid-like;
          we would play that game later
We expected the snappers: their warrior shells

lining the mouth of the house like teeth, the mouths of
fire
and gargoyles
that arching cathedral
Yet the snappers had done their worst –
 left haunting silence of dull rain &
                        the smell of rotting wood
We navigated the boat through the front passage –
saw furniture & bottles, bobbing
This could be fun, living in the house of floating
chairs –
perhaps a tea party was in order. As I paddled toward
the kitchen I pulled the oar against a sheet
billowing and pillowish
As I pulled the heavy laundry like the old
washer woman in the movies – the sheet slipped away and
-there was the creased waxy face, your mouth shaped in an O
and I wondered if you had anything left to say

# LEONARD AND MAUDE AT CROOKED POND

My brother and I rowed that awful rowing toward the south end of
Crooked Pond. Where the snapping turtles live underneath the
water lilies.

A little boy had run to the end of the Miller's dock a year before and
jumped in and could not swim.

Red & blue paint flaked from the ancient rowboat into murky depths.
I bailed from the boat bottom with the half milk jug.

You pulled with the left oar and I pulled with the right.
We rowed past the rotted hemlock trees and the old rope swing.

I wanted to go to the place where those two toads, Leonard and
Maude, were friends. A land of cardboard castles built in the grainy
sand at the water's edge, in the twinkling light of the water, the shore
wooded with evergreens.

Remember when the woman in the white house by the water lilies
washed her hair with shampoo?

Suds floated toward the north end for days, and musk turtles came to
shore. Sunfish went belly-up with soapy scales, washed to a small
beach of redemption.

But Leonard and Maude drank tea on the shore, holding crisp china cups in their webby hands.

# STONY CREEK BEACH

Soft sensibility of sand and ocean cold,
the water like little pins on my skin
during the Thanksgiving day plunge.
Islands dot the horizon, overturned
thimbles full of water.

I moved here to be closer to my mother,
and I rush into the cold water with her
every year at this time. You
set your blue striped towels down

on the sea wall by the water's edge,
and slide off your flip flops from your
rough feet. The pebbles and small grains
of sand rub at your toes and heels.

You reach for your mother's hand
and yell, "We can do this" into the frigid air.
You hold hands as you run into the water,
emitting high-pitched screams as if this

can combat the cold. Your hands separate
and you each dive in headfirst. And you
wonder whether things will get bad again.

You are swallowing mouthfuls of
brackish water, the comfort of salt,
incandescent net of ocean. Moorings
ding with wind

sound and seaweed wraps against your calves
threatening to pull you under,
the black muck pulls at your heels,

You see scales of bluefish and wish to
hold them in your hands, to know the sharp cut
of the green blue ridges and white half moon.

# PENZANCE POINT

Grammy Rose took us to *High Society*
and *Pirates of Penzance* at the College Playhouse
in Falmouth, Massachusetts.
I squirmed in the seat but wanted to sing with the pirates.
Then came intermission, ginger ale with cherries and syrup.

I wore a pink ruffled dress, matching Mary Jane shoes and when
Grammy Rose hugged me there was a smell of moth balls and
formaldehyde. I remembered the basement, Grandpa
Rose with his aquariums, glass boxes of frogs and dissection kits,
the poorly designed architecture of the house on Crosby Lane,
and the day my brother fell into the lily pond on the hill.

Father told me there was a Penzance Point in Woods Hole
and we could see it from Devil's Foot Cove.
Pirates lived there, he said,
with their treasure among the trees and their tents.
They harbored their ships to the back of the point.
I wanted to plunder and pillage with these folk,
these swordsman and swashbucklers, have my brother
walk the plank, and drape myself in tourmaline and rubies.
When I drove to Penzance years later all I could find were
the stately mansions, primly cut lawns,
cracked oyster shell driveways.

# WHAT IF HER MOTHER WERE ANDROMEDA?

What if she could just hang
you in the battered night
for awhile, close
to the slivered moon, against
the red-white meteor showers?

Above the craggy rocks where
the self-effacing green waters churn.

Your white dress billowing among
the spray of stars, in the deafening waves
of space, arms stretched wide.

Now you crucify yourself on the North Star.

When she was little she studied your frail
depths & brittle trajectories; should she still
apologize for taking up space in the world?

Who will save her from errant sea monsters
and overzealous suitors?

Not you: your ecliptic distance and dragon
scaled moon no safety net.

# TOO MUCH OF WATER

Muscles striated against the bone

Blue and green bottles, floating shards, sound the tone

I lay face down—legs & fingers splayed

Fire the kiln – red & black & char

There I lay with sixty white pills like stars

Concentric circles of sound echo the sky

Wings of Jazz Icarus - a wax dragonfly

With sea glass stones in my pocket as turquoise water

rises I try to fill the hollow

With scotch & visible bones & men of different sizes

I fear the silence outside –

I fear the sopranos' shrill within

Yet incantation of night stars and sky begin to calm the din

## THE NIGHT HE WAS BORN: A PROLOGUE

*for J.R.*


The planet tilts that deep night on 227 Acacia Avenue,

as I writhe in duck & bunny sheets

below glow-in-the-dark constellations

                                        a mass of limegreen stars and glue


my hair matted, snail shell curls pasted

to my forehead.

                                                  —————


My father comes in at eleven,

He lifts me from the sweat stain I left on

the sheets

                                        the shape of Cape Cod


ebbing, drying into the smaller islands of

Naushon, Cuddyhunk reaching towards the bay,

and I grab his blue cotton shirt with both fists.

                                                  —————


The mommy-daddy room smells of strange salted sweat.

All I see:

Skinny white legs splayed on the bed.

hands white against the comforter,

constellated with oranges and yellows,

my mother's face not her own
but made of heavy breaths and sounds.
Legs shake and push something
through, red and wet, come with its own scream,
a new foreign thing, a brother.

———————

Legs shake again and push something through,
Red, white and wet but without its own scream
then, a mass of silver tongs and basins

———————

My father tells me they will bury
the placenta in the backyard
underneath the lemon tree, waxed green and yellow
where I will watch it dissolve into the ground.

# MATISSE: JAZZ ICARUS, 1943

Limbs leaning towards drowning night.
Static motion: the wingless body of Icarus.
The blue-black sphere of faceless notes.
Chromatic chords cut at sharp angles.

Pour the music of the swift eighth notes
into the solitary, sterile figure, unfulfilled.
What have you gained by loss of limbs?
Hands and feet immersed in melody.

Yellow beats and red center of sound.
Eternity in constellated improvisation.
Slave to the staff of impending dawn.
The crescendo echoes against the frame.

Let the liquid night infuse immortality.
Orpheus's incantation of sound and stars.

# DEVIL'S FOOT COVE

In Woods Hole, Massachusetts,
my father paddles through the water,
ribs of his canoe digging into mine.
Masts creak the harbor and buoys, blue, white and rust,
ding with wind sound. Children jump from tugboats,
orange and peeling. My father points to tall masts,
short masts, teaching us the difference
between sloops and schooners.
He speaks of times he and cousin Jimmy would
swim to the Cove, rum bottles tied to their big toes.
We shore by the sluice, swim in, let the water carry us, rushing.
My father calls to me, he wants help organizing the ropes and
paddles. I run

to the other side of the cove, crab grass and beach roses

scratch as my mother and I search for places to hide among
the rocks. Later, I race my brother along the spit,
cutting my toe on a broken scallop shell, red
against the white sand.

# HOW TO HYPNOTIZE A LOBSTER

Step 1. Post a sarcastic profile to Match.com. Write that you know half the alphabet, but other than that, you bring nothing to the table.

Step 2. Your first date is at Harvest restaurant in New Haven before going to see Mathilda at the Schubert Theatre. The service at the restaurant is atrocious, but you will know upon first meeting you that you can implicitly be yourself.

Step 3. Joke about lining your pockets with appetizers and snacks for later and how you had entered an "all you can eat shrimp competition" with a co-worker at Yale. He won't seem bothered by your brand of weird and will seem to get you.

Step 4. The performance of Mathilda is flawless, and you will be sold by second dinner that evening at Barcelona restaurant. Kiss him underneath the lamp post before getting into your car outside of Calhoun hall. The lamplight flickers through the elm leaves.

Step 5. Go camping at Blue Shutter beach in Rhode Island. Forget to wear sunblock. Jump in the waves and eat clam chowder for dinner at the Clam Shack down the road. Your skin will be hot and all you taste is sun and salt.

Step 6. After a year together, get a puppy. Make sure she is a rescue; half lab, half hound. Call her Fiona, 'Fee' for short. She will be the most neurotic dog you have ever met.

Step 7. Move to a house by the beach in Connecticut. In the winter, you can feel the wind coming through the siding. Fee will run five miles on the beach every morning, with the wind in her ears.

Step 8. Move to Blacksburg, Virginia for work. Go to the farmer's market, Claytor Lake. Host summer parties in the backyard with craft beer and a slip 'n' slide.

Step 9. Buy fresh lobsters from the fish market – Ask if he knows how to hypnotize a lobster? He'll smile and say, "Yes." Flip your lobsters upside down on the marble countertops—slowly massage the red warrior tails, lobsters rest on their heads, the water boils.

Step 10. Take your lobsters from headstand position and toss them into the pot, kiss your future husband.

# FLIGHT OF ICARUS

I knew what I was doing,
lifting over crosshatched stones,
grey and red, seams like tributaries
wondering what lived in the spaces

between those graveled stones, twists
of light on the wind, saturated and
soft against my back, I
was a black cut-out figure

against the sky and wondered what
gnarled hand had woven this dream?
I saw the beveled labyrinth and minotaur.
The yellow scales of eagles' feet, talons

blunted by wayward rocks.
The wax was fresh and the feathers
second hand. I'm sorry, Father.
I remember the month

I was sick as a boy, hot with fever and
you took me down to the ocean's rim
so I could breathe again, and we sat,
trying to stop the waves.

But this day, I flew, feathered with fear,
clutching the broken compass
you had given me on my sixteenth birthday,
the antique glass cracked open,
the needle bent. North, South,
East, West, blending to one.

I flew towards what was warm
and what I felt was good.

The wax melted across my shoulders, my back,
Finally I had made a choice that was mine.

I fell past the cool waters into
seaweedy depths of kelp and coral.

The sun made sense.
The sea made sense.

## PERMISSION I

I do not have that yellowed slip.
I have not forged your cramped signature.
I do not recall cracked abalone shells and abandon.
Do I have your permission to take up space
in this monochrome, sharpened world?

I saw a dead deer today on the side of the road. I
didn't want to look at its fractured face,
the mottled, bloodied fur, the disfigurement.
This lack of permission, me never knowing if I am rooted, is
this enough, can it be? Is it cotton balls and dyed flowers,

is it wringing myself out with starvation? is it?
Is it the hating? the loathing? Permission to be here or not here. I
write and cannot write. The muddled sleep is easier – it is best. I
dream about how our feet never touch the earth,
the dirt anymore, we have soles and sidewalks,

tires and concrete roadways pooling,
incandescent in the sun.

# PART II

"All writers are vain, selfish and lazy, and at the very bottom of their motives lies a mystery. Writing a book is a horrible, exhausting struggle, like a long bout of some painful illness. One would never undertake such a thing if one were not driven by some demon whom one can neither resist nor understand."

*~ George Orwell*

# THE TAXIDERMIST OF POETRY



I take your words and drain them
insert the needle through the thin nose of the S
Pull graymatter like Egyptians
*I'm happy now – I want you to be happy for me.*

Columns of large words will cry to be wrapped and bound-
"Make us small forever -
Like dainty feet. "
Unspeakable words –

the ones
I am afraid of
want to be wrapped
in white, painted
with unlocked daisies

*A man has needs.*
I take your words and bleed them, fill them with sand and tiny stitches.

*And    But*
Conjunctions wish for enlargement-
"Fill us with sand!"
they scream
pump us
up beyond adequate
size - you do
not know
how it feels
to be
invisible.

## PERMISSION II
*after Elizabeth Bishop*


So you become the searing blue of pain,
the fractured shade of never knowing.
A thesaurus of paralysis like the crocodile's
eye placed in the cracked green wall.
You stand at the lip of the ocean trying
to stop the waves with a curved tree
branch, the necessary green blossoms.
You become an affliction so weighted
to the center that hums like a swarm
 of white bees in your abdomen.
 You mourn but do not know what
 you are mourning for
in the dusk, dim light of childhood.
You wonder when anything will be
enough to stop the many speckled
voices, weaving drops of dew on the
windowpane, when you will stop
hearing the color red,
its vibrant staccato sound.
You wish for an antidote, many steps
away from this sharp topography.
You cannot stop the dreams of the
winched salt and striated
memories, like flickers of silverfish
around your ankles, the
many layers of the sea wrapping
your body, giving you
a permission to float.
This is nothing like redemption.

You say to yourself: seven days
and you'll be thirty-two years old.
The same age your mother was
when she had you
in San Diego, California. You
remember the lemon tree and

the white blossoms.
Your father buried the placenta
underneath it after your brother
was born that tar burnt night.
The house on Acacia Street

was small and red,
you remember a red
terracotta walkway,
a backyard with
a swingset, half-paved.
You remember a blue rain
slicker and an umbrella –
but not the rain or its warmth.
You remember an earthquake, the
street rolling outside like a serpent.
Calls from your parents to stand in the doorway,
but never remember feeling trapped
the way you do now.
The ocean was permeable
then, the streets were permeable
in memory it always seems easier,
like the pictures hanging on your
mother's wall.
You running naked, wrapped in seaweed
blonde hair in pigtails, smiling, eating
fistfuls of sand,
You asking permission to be an "I"
 and testing the limits of sand and sky
and ocean, the flights of gulls
and there is nothing to claim because
This is nothing like redemption.

# BRITISH IMPERIALISM: MAD AS A BOX OF FROGS

*"You, my love, are mad as a box of frogs."*
Good sir, what sort of frogs, how many? Tree frogs? Bullfrogs?
*"Definitely not bullfrogs: too static."*
And what sort of box? Shoe box? Hat box?
Are there holes so the frogs may breathe?
  *"It's like 350 Costa Rican tree frogs in a box designed for tiny shoes."*

Do you think you can just wage battle and then break for tea at 4pm?
Follow your compass in any direction and plant a tattered flag?
Do you think this is proper? With your blue wool
sweater-vests and impeccably styled blonde hair, short
and soft with a slight curl?
Is it fine to create slave camps in Antigua if it doesn't affect tea time?
Please, sir. Cease and desist.
If I hear one more time, "O, you are such an American,"
I will fill my pockets with damp tea bags and when I see you
I will throw them in your general direction.
No conjugation without representation.
Sadly, I no longer find Monty Python as funny.
I will not miss your high-pitched laugh, somewhat ladylike.
So take your mad box of frogs, boxes of tea, and silly flags.
Ignorance and arrogance is bad foreign policy.
Also, this is true.
You asked me once, "If I didn't have this accent would you like me as much?"
And of course my answer was, "No."

# MATISSE: LES FAUVES, 1905

Blue smears of paint and striated abandon
Who framed this fearful beast of land and scales?
Feathered sea of cerulean and mustard honey, and I
wonder how did you paint my madness?

Echoing the rotting planks as they splinter
with weight. Sharpened talons scratch and gnaw
past the temple flower sounds
I peel the white skin from my heels

A bumblebee of constant sound and thin wings
Past the dirt and the mulch and the smell of dry grasses I
wonder what that is or was
These mounds of flesh & swirls of yellow

I can't be as I once was or would be
Let the thinking stop
Let the pounding stop
The thundering stop
The squawk of gulls, the marriage plot

the veiled curtains whispering in the breeze
the grains of sand suddenly blue mountains
Is it possible to live as a wild thing once we are contained?
My feet never touch the earth

I could dig through layers of concrete and steel with this teaspoon
impractical caterwauling
the curve on the mottled wooden chair
stringy feathers saturated with briny water

talons of disease and marrow
myriad of cobblestone arteries and wingless flies
the rolls of my flesh disgust me and I wonder
if I can shed them like a second skin and be scrubbed clean

and what is a sense of place: a smell, a taste, a sound?
the train flutes in the background the horn a recorder
What if what is does not want to become more?

# 3 DON'TS FOR BEAUTIFUL GIRLS

I. Don't Undervalue or Overvalue Your Beauty.


Mother poured your bottles down the sink,

Mother never knew if you would be passed out

on the chaise longue when she returned from school.

Now she finds my bottles in the wicker hamper, pours


them down the sink, finds me passed out

on the featherbed, blonde hair pooling around me,

between clean blue sheets because this

is where I feel safe.


The frayed composition book of your journal is entitled "Poems?"

Your handwriting loops evenly, your "Fs" like infinity signs.

You were a fair poet, writing of love and Edna St. Vincent Millay.

In your scrapbooks, you preserved postcards, playbills

and telegrams asking you to dances or to the lake.

You pasted a half-smoked Camel cigarette and a smooth

Flat stone around a postcard of the Narrows River, East Brady, PA

you wrote to Andy, in pencil on August 23$^{rd}$, 1934.


In pictures on mother's mantle you are beautiful and sad.

Mother said you had aspirations to model and act but

but attended Cornell instead to study Psychology,

all those abnormalities.

You met your husband your sophomore year.

I found a newspaper clipping you had pasted in the early pages

of the journal, written by a Hollywood producer. He listed

"10 Don'ts for Beautiful Girls" and I wondered if you followed them?


II. Don't permit the whirl of social life to rob you of your youth and

beauty before your time.


Step 1. Find a dishy man at rehab.


Step 2. Hope he is just as broken as you.

Flirt and make eyes across the red barn.

Sneak up behind him in the coffee line, whisper in his ear, "Come here often?"

He'll smile that 6'2 Cape Cod smile and say, "Sure do."


Step 3. Start writing him eighth grade love notes with Emily Dickinson

quotes like "Dwell in possibility" littering the page.

Pass the notes to him in chapel,

while sitting on the wooden benches.

Try to catch his eye in the laundry room.

Knit compulsively – the green boucle yarn.

He'll ask if what you are knitting is for him?

Say Yes~

It is a tube top or

a thong.

Step 4. Kiss him at the coke machine, kiss him at the lamp post- don't care if you get caught, Kiss him beneath the stars to the left of the barn in the freezing cold tangled beneath his blue-checked shirt – your skin touching his – patches of your back touching the roots the grass, the pebbles, the dirt, the cold – he'll try to pull the Carhartt jacket around your writhing bodies.

Step 5. Get asked to leave rehab because you and your man are a danger to the community. Remember: "There is no fraternization."

Step 6. Listen to his warm south Boston accent. Make plans to meet
in Newport, Pocasset, on the Vineyard,
at The Flying Horses, win the brass ring.
Drive in the sun to Katama beach with his hands between your knees.
Talk about getting matching Native American tattoos in Vineyard Haven.
Don't get them.

Step 7. The next night, relapse together.

III. Don't drink or smoke. Beauty first depends upon excellent health.

Step 1. Wake up in rehab dreaming of blue bottles.

Step 2. Wonder how you got here again?

Step 3. Lie in fresh sheets and smell regret and guilt.

Step 4. Don't look for dishy men. They can't help you now.

Step 5. Smoke cigarettes at every fresh air break. Blow smoke rings
    toward the sun-dappled trees on the other side of the street.
    You are not allowed to walk further than the lamp-post.

Step 6. Dream of bathing in champagne, holding a glistening martini glass

Step 7. Blank stamps of memory will come back to you, but you
    cannot drink them down.

Step 8. Be ready for omens. Ask for a hawk, a seagull or a robin to
    fly past when you feel shaky.

Step 9. Learn you are two blocks from the beach.

Step 10. Pack up all your belongings.
    Unpack.

Step 11. Flirt with the cutest guy in rehab. You've nicknamed him Vladimir

Step 12. Walk to the beach and look for the echo of
    gulls and crashing waves. Wonder how
    you are supposed to fall in love with yourself?
    Is it easier when you are knee-deep in the ocean

between the blue-grained spheres of water and sky?
Snails are migrating to shore because that's where the
hope is, with the silt and sunfish,
with two cranes landing in shallow water, a
ladybug with 7 dots on her wings,
a rose quartz stone in your hand.


You decide the ocean can take it all.
You decide you are enough.

# HALF MOON BAY

Dark sensibility of sand and ocean cold
On our January skin. Naked as the moon darkens, you
    cover me with a rain of spray.

    You said, "I want to always be honest."
I said, "There is a difference between being honest
    and being an asshole." Your fingers

    nimble but thick, press steel strings
of the guitar. Your black hair illumined by the reds,
    yellows and blue woven into your

    Peruvian blanket against the sand.
The night I broke, you were three hours late and I
    was already drunk. I tried to be honest,

    I'm sure there was a better place
than the beer-stained couch, but I hope that hurt you
    more, you left saying

    "I do not like where this conversation
is going." I remember our fourth date when we went skinny-
    dipping at Half Moon Bay. Two in the

morning as we stripped down, me self-
conscious. You wondered why I was slowing, you had
seen me already. Two bodies naked in

the moon-glow. I miss your coffee
breath and the leather-sweat smell of the shoes you
refused to throw away. I miss your

black sheets and black and white
photographs. I miss the soft and shiny curve of your
left ear, the pearly interiority of

a conch shell. I miss the continuous
sound of the drowning ocean. But I let you go—now
leave you in the sand at the bay.

# AIR GUITAR

Summer of 1975, my father invites my mother to his summerhouse on Cape Cod at Crooked Pond. The clouds are knitted into the pool-blue sky as they laugh and swim in the brackish water of the pond, which is exactly ten steps from the house. The sunfish flicker in the shallows. They swim to the center of the pond, float on their backs and look towards the grainy shore and brown-shingled cottage with white- trimmed windows. They swim in closer and my father disappears beneath the surface of the green water and grabs my mother by the waist and lifts her up. They laugh as she splashes down into the water. Their feet rub together and she dunks him and they kiss underwater.

That night, on the screened-in porch, my father plays the flamenco guitar for my mother by lantern-light. The black lace of the tree branches reflect on the moonlit pond water, and my mother stretches out on the Indian blanket woven with swirling blues, reds and yellows.

Summer of 1984, I run around wildly in my wet blue polka-dotted bathing suit singing, *Can't Get No Satisfaction* and playing the air guitar. I open the creaky French doors to the porch and hop on the guest beds, digging my toes into the fresh cotton quilt; sand tickles the bottom of my feet. I swing my arms, circularly strumming in the musky afternoon air and my blonde, wet curls bounce against my shoulders. I jump down off the bed and run back into the living room, leaving sandy footprints on the maple floor.

My damp hair curls mermaid-like around my face and I shimmy in front of the dust-covered mirror, laughing at my reflection.

Summer of 1986, my father, hair still dark and body lean, sits in the sturdy oak chair with the honey-colored guitar in his arms. The classical guitar is banded to his shoulder by the red, green and pink- colored strap he bought in Peru. He plays "Puff the Magic Dragon," and my brother and I sit at his leathery feet singing along. My father's fingers, nimble but thick, press down the steel strings and the warm, round notes hang in the air above my head. There is a warmth in my body down to my toes.

Summer of 1990, my father is driving the family to Cape Cod to visit our grandmother. I sit in the front seat singing along to the radio, thighs sticky from the humidity. My father, hair graying and waistline expanding, turns his head swiftly and shakes my leg. He tells me to "Shut up and stop singing." He says I'm tone deaf just like Mom and I should get my dirty feet off the dashboard. My mom and brother sit in silence in the back of the silver Caravan.

Summer of 1994, my first real boyfriend, Jim, incessantly plays "While My Guitar Gently Weeps." He sits on the edge of his bed, plaid shirt unbuttoned, head down, brown hair swept over his eyes. He brings me daisies, writes me poetry and I think he belongs to another decade. He leaves for college at the end of that summer and we never speak again.

Summer of 1997, my father moves out of our yellow farmhouse on Shell Beach Road.

Summer of 1998, the phone rings. It is my father. I take the white portable phone from its cradle on the wall and walk out onto the splintering screened-in porch. The green paint is crackling from the wall and my brother's cigarette butts overflow the chipped flowerpots. My father is calling to invite me to his wedding on Cape Cod. It is his third marriage. I tell him I have to work.

Summer of 1999, I'm accepted to the a capella group at school. I open my mouth and sing into the rafters at the Congregational Church, wearing a lavender silk gown.

Summer of 2001, it is a rough, stormy day with drops of rain on the window. This kind of day used to comfort me but now does not. I want to move from my curdle-sheeted bed but cannot. My brother told me there's something wrong with me and I'm all fucked up. He said if I really wanted to I could get up and stop being depressed. I hardly hear my mother sit down beside me or feel the clasp of her hand. The silence suspends hollowly between us, invading the clutter of my room. I still have not unpacked after coming home from college two months ago. My dust-covered guitar sits unplayed in the corner since I received it on my eighteenth birthday. I know four chords.

My mother's hands seem worn and wise. The blood pulses

swiftly to her fingertips in elevated tributaries. It is a swift movement I want in my own limbs. Her nails are short, filed and economical. They are efficient, which is everything I feel I am not. The unpolished half-moons of my mother's fingernails stand out against the grayness of the room. My mother's creased hands, the lines and crosshatchings remind me of a nautical chart.

Summer of 2002, I bury my head in my boyfriend's black sheets and pillowcases, breathing in sour, pungent boy smell mixed with oak cologne. There is something wonderful about being alone in his room, waiting for him to get off work and crawl into bed with me. The glowing red lights of the clock flash 2:01 am into the darkness. He should be home around 3. There's a secrecy, an indulgence to being in his bed alone. I turn on the lights and look at the room. Black and white photos of his year abroad hang against the peeling walls. He smiles down at me from a photograph, shirtless against a beat-up bus parked by a building at the kibbutz. I turn off the light and spread my limbs across the queen-size bed and make snow angel movements in the sheets. Shadows shift across my face and the humid air traces my exposed skin, and I wait for him to come home.

Summer of 2003, my roommate and I start a band called *Lilt* and play covers of the Indigo Girls and Pat Benetar at Café Nine.

Summer of 2007, I no longer feel safe in our apartment in San Francisco close to the bay. Unplayed guitars and empty bottles litter the living room. I try not to feel that puffed up emptiness, feathered failure of holes punched in the walls and unwashed blue dishes.

# NED THE NIGHT HERRING

*for L.J.*


From here I climb the skull of the rock

fountain & no one is here.

Where I eat blue flowers like air.

The sky's crown of lights: a flash flood.

I search for the brass handle with rough

grass beneath my summer feet.

The light at the lamp post glows

turquoise, white, & green with heat

& I feel the ribs of the

canoe on the rough water.

Tonight is my last performance with

Ned the Night Herring &

I float in the rainy sky's crown of

light: a wet firefly.

The blue hydrangeas scream

soft with texture &

I wish to drudge & scull

the sea for bits of broken compass.

# LITTLE PIPPI

I desire a chauffeur and 10 top-hatted mechanics,

the smell of diesel, black under cracked nails.

Your ears and lips smell the smoky morning exhaust,

and in Woods Hole, Massachusetts, Florence Rose feeds her box of frogs.

But what of trains and cars and broken steering?

My mother fiendishly texts OMG

If I had loved you enough would my body still be next to his?

Are we in glass houses with sea glass stones?

That day the farmhouse cracked open

Mother flew to the ceiling, arranging pots and pans to catch the rain.

Little Pippi was there in a life jacket:

She will have 8 husbands by the time she dies,

smoothing pennies on bendable train tracks.

I'll have to love them all to love you the best.

## RED

Red is for liability, the ruby, the incendiary flame:

The red roof tiles, that red, in the trail of silt;

Fireworks, the red of distemper;

The red of wine, the tracks of sediment;

The consecrated red of open veins;

Manipulative red, the red of coals;

The striated red, showing what is lost;

The red of the kiln, a smudge of terra cotta and char;

The red of what is dependable; because I no longer am.

Red of poppies, red of lacquered nails;

The red of fire alarms, the blood beneath the skin;

The red of fall leaves, their curled edges;

Red giant, bright against a blackened night;

Red is for evading responsibility;

The red of bruised skin, the extinguisher, the pirate's sky.

# PART III

"And your very flesh shall be a great poem and have the richest fluency not only in its words but in the silent lines of its lips and face and between the lashes of your eyes and in every motion and joint of your body."

~*Walt Whitman*

# OMISSION

She won't go to those coping meetings
with a bunch of whiny knitters.
I tell her it is the information that she
leaves out, that is so dangerous.
She speaks fleetingly of her mother passed
out drunk on the flowered chaise longue
whenever she returned home from school.
And now she watches us struggle, but she
does not believe it is a disease.
She tells us, "just a little more exercise, a hot
steamy shower. Maybe you just need a vacation."
And she'll fly to Florida to rescue my brother from the
hospital, he won't have been lucid for six days,
and he'll finally wake up and they'll decorate the
house, the white lights for Christmas which was
missed, and they'll sit in the sunshine and feed the
chickens, Belina and Tillie, and she'll send me a video
clip and the light will be speckled, and it will be as it
was.

# THE FALL OF ICARUS, 1943

And you fell, my dear son, through that sunburned night.

The feathered music had stopped & the wax had melted.

Your limbs fell limp & the stars, no longer your friends.

I wondered what I could have done differently.


I do not blame your father – he did the best he could.

But all he knew was how to build and admonish,

lean on laws of science and hide in theorems.

I know the law of gravity is never enough.


You are safe in the ocean now,

cradled in wax and kelp.

No one ever taught you to listen.

So how could we expect you to?


So, rest my darling, in the blue waters, among the coral.

Let the waves and sirens take you.

# Q: WHAT IF LOVE WERE A WHITE PARROT

A: No, it is a cup of blood & cracked oyster shells,
an empty train on bended tracks, pooling oil

Q: What if love were the ear of the teacup?
A: No, Cooling memory and desire, a croquet mallet left in the sun

Q: What if love were the curved tines of the fork?
A: No, Coffee stains & grounds left in the shapes of small islands at
the bottom of my cup

Q: What if love were rusting buoys? Unanswered wind?
A: No, Flattened pennies warming on the train tracks

Q: What if love were the yellowed scales of the sunfish, the glint of
the fishing lure?
A: No, The half-bailed rowboat creaking the harbor

Q: What if love were a car without a steering column?
A: No, Striated branches of hydrangea blues and greens

Q: What if love were the stone sound of the flowers?
A: No, A grasshopper pinned against the dirty glass

Q: Is love this empty hollow of the robin? Earthworm in
mouth running among the eggplants?
A: No, What if I can no longer stand this emptiness? A heaviness of
puffed up feather and pointed beaks, flying in unison, wishing to
move but stuck, this hopping pattern of anger, in dried grasses. Black
beaks and hooded eyes, the brown and grey of feathers, this adjacent
loneliness.

Q: Is love the bloated curve of my stomach &
your scarred white thigh?
A: No, It is a cigarette burn in the small of my arm
the berry-shaped bruise on the small of your back

Q: What if love were simply a red-beaked duck
roaming the pebbled beach?
A: Is it traveling in a pack of three
against the blue water?

# THE NAUTICAL CHARTS OF SILENCE

30 degrees latitude: That day I wished to lie

face-down under glass

over crosshatchings of maps,

a strange topography.

My legs and fingers splayed,

reaching for Cape Cod Bay and

the island of Naushon.


90 degrees longitude:

I wish to be filled with sand,

for map pins to pierce my heels— never to move.


At a lesser depth, in New Haven, CT

the vampire boy from

down the hall constantly follows me

but I find him flattering.


60 degrees latitude:

I am allowed outdoor privileges,

cry to my mother *I do not belong here*

but I fear the silence outside;

It is fathomless & the sextant broken.

# RED POPPY, MOON AND WISHBONE

I. Breaking the Wishbone

Fill the mouths with glazed clay
Glazed red poppy red

Cones of lilac and hyacinth drown in the mulch
Ankles roll among the roots, splitting
Nails to the half moons
Some monocled man talks of cruel months

The transparency of green wings
Snap in the heat

Arms bent back, beyond pain
Cut away at the midsection where it arcs
Striated muscle and marrow
Another bespectacled man says this is the exact location
of the soul

A white canopy bed hangs between two tall redwood trees and
I wish to break the wishbone hidden in the velvet corners

II. Moon after the Wreck,  1901


That night my great grandmother stepped past the
water into whiteness.
Black jetties bled the boat into the sand.
Seams of tide brought bodies down.
She wanted a story that was not hers,
away from the winched salt, bruised sails, green water
He was waiting at the trees beyond the grainy shore.
That night it rained white petals to black branches
The year my grandmother was born, wooden timbers
pushed through the sand,
My great grandmother walked to the edge,
carrying her baby, the tide so low,
the sirens silent,
the moon brightened.


III. Dogwood Forts


In Wellfleet, Massachusetts, my woven poppy quilt frays where
our bodies angle in the sand.
Your elbow digs into my thigh and I play with the thick hair
on your forearm –
The cove is lined with silt, flickers with sunfish.

Laurel woods are drenched in rain –

Tulips heavy to the center with water.

At the dogwood forts and evergreen tepees,

we sew skirts of waxy leaves by the streams edged with stones and clay.

We smooth our pennies on the train tracks.


IV. I Do Not Kid About Fire, Sharks & Knives


                  Circle the fire in glass
      jars as wax cherries              hiss & crackle
              A little bowl of
                Fireworks
     I wonder if the spoon envies
                the sharp marks her brothers
           make on the
            world?
In Napili Kai that day
          the man emerged from the waves,
                    his autopsied calf
        red on white sand

# AT MY FIRST BAR JOB IN SAN FRANCISCO

black apron, Harpoon bottle opener and

silver wine key, I began pretending

Never knowing who I was

That I came from different countries.

I'd run my hand over the globe each night,

tracing the different topographies

a Finish accent, and English accent,

"allo Guvnor."

One day I was from the Midwest

dreaming of bruised fields and Minnesota,

the next day I would find myself

using a Russian accent while pouring

well vodka. It always became difficult,

with repeat customers. Sal from the

investment firm, the Republican

trying to act in commercials, proudly bringing

in the box of Milkbone dog biscuits with his

face on it. My boss would catch me, always

puzzled, "the wheels are coming off, Ms. Rose."

"Lo siento, senor" I would reply

And then I began to run

into regulars on the street.

"Hey it's the Finnish girl." "No, she's from

France." I was reminded of my little brother,

running around the house

in onesie pajamas, pointing at himself
yelling the lines from a Muzzy commercial,
"Je suis la jeune fille." There was a delight,
a success in being someone else, in never
being seen among the blue-green bottles,
the shards of glass, the rows of candles
and caged tequila bottles. It was in that bar,
44 Union Street, I met my ex-husband,
thick Cape Cod accent and progressive
alcoholism, the English accent was his
favorite, "allo Poppet."
I remember spending nights
never really knowing each other
in my studio apartment

$4^{th}$ floor walk up in Nob Hill, San Francisco
steep hills of concrete
a box of wine and incendiary accents.

# 21 SHELL BEACH ROAD

The yellow farmhouse sits at the top of the hill,
that steep hill that is always the price of going home.
The troll neighbor lives across the street,
brings bushels of strawberries as offerings.

The neighbor to the right walks daily
to the beach, swinging his cane at my dogs.
He is a meteorologist of some sort
with a shrill wife behind window glass.
My brother and his friends play croquet,
in tuxedos, get the dog stoned, and
call her Winky, watch her
bury marshmallows in the backyard.

From the farmhouse we have a view of
Long Island sound, and Leetes Island across the cove.
We swim from the craggy rocks in the summer
cutting our feet on the jagged shells.
I taught Winky to swim from those rocks,
she will now hop on the back of my father's
windsurfer and float about.

Inside the farmhouse, I remember a coldness.
Built in 1853, it creaks in the November wind.
The pine beams in the ceilings leak when it
rains too hard. Mother aligns dented pots and pans
to catch the drippage in the attic and the living room.

My father leaves post-it notes reminding us to shut
off the lights and to be quiet in the mornings when
we get ready for school.
It is the most communication I have with him all month.

My father leaves that house when I am 15.
The grasses begin to overgrow and the upperdeck
begins to chip and peel white paint.
My brother and I have bonfires in the back, near the
evergreens. Litter the lawn with broken bottles.
The troll neighbor increases his visits with bushels of
strawberries.

# 13 WAYS OF LOOKING AT A CROCODILE

*after Wallace Stevens*


I
An eye like a candle flame,
Incandescent crocodile scales of abandon
moving in the brush.

II
Three self-determining shades of green,
A solid bamboo tree,
At the base, three crocodiles.

III
The crocodile opens its mouth,
fanning yellow teeth,
At the shallow edge of the river.

IV
The sandpaper feet of a crocodile
move almost silently,
as a fractured tooth drops from
the mouth of the crocodile.

V
Looking for crocodiles
The beauty of indecisions,
the snapping teeth of false judgment,
The crocodile feeding
Or just before.

VI
Sunlight fills the round window
Of the taxidermist's shop.
The shadow of the crocodile
immobile, under
glinting shingles of skin,
underscored in shadow.

VII
A child buries his sister in the sand,
her brother has shaped her a
grainy crocodile tail.

VIII
I know the undercurrents
of your tone.
I know the crocodile is consumed
With what is said and not said.

IX
When the crocodile sleeps,
the green wall cracks and fissures,
and I am full of leathered fear.

X
A petulant waitress and a
crocodile beneath a
thin veneer of waves where
blue is for emptiness, the smoke signal,
the glass eye.

XI
The grateful crocodile sheds his
scales without remorse.

XII
A glass case of golden crocodile miniatures
arranged snout to tail,
glinting in the winter sun.

XIII
It was summer all afternoon.
A wave of feathered heat.
The crocodile lays, shining
the muddy bank.

## SOLAR ELLIPSIS

The sun is the father of mathematics and closed curves,
or from the Greek a warm "falling short"…
At the end of September, I doubt my chart is true,
I've collected Donne's compass, the broken foot
What is erect will never come home
Feeble crosshatching of lines and astral charts,

I wonder if the sun is jealous of the constellations,
their little pinpoints of light?

The sun can find no comfort
No true place
Can you draw or sketch or indel?
I've collected the signposts
Twisted twice around in the woods
Seen the same place for the first time
I run my fingers across the globe, track the elevated mountains,
the tributaries and impenetrable oceans, but
still no true place
I want a heated geography that is not mine
The sun is the father of mathematics and closed curves.

# TANKA INFINITY

The lilac tree buds
The dishes are never washed
An empty town blooms

A woodpecker and a swallow
A consternation of song

A lonely gravesite
of empty rush and grasses
A field mouse nests here

An open archway defers
To bell flowers sounds above

The blonde hair straw-like, a
noose that is all you need to
know.

# SATISFY

To satisfy, I lie head to
toe with my sisters.
Sometimes we spoon in
our dark home of the
divided metal basket.

I awake when the light
shines through the crack
in the morning. I
wonder what type of
soak I will have today?

Sometimes it's a hot tea
bath or blackened
coffee dip, depending
on your mood. I like to
be swirled in circular
motions, I feel useful.

I like the warmth
of your hand against my
silver skin. The lemon
soap smell on your
jagged fingernails.

I'm jealous of my
brothers, spear-headed
and blunt. I envy the
sharpness of the marks
they make on the
cutting board of the
world.

# HIS

His hair was wisps of dandelion tufts

and his eyes were blue robin's eggs left by their mother

and his bite was a clipped passenger side mirror

His nostrils were two seeds of the unripened pear

And his mouth was drunken marital vows

and his smile was the unraveling lanyard woven at summer camp

and his tongue was the scales of sunfish

and his laugh was the rustle of venetian blinds

He snored, and it was incendiary devices

and his arguments were narwhals escaped from captivity

and his neck was a pitcher of milk

and his Adam's apple was a dolphin fin

and his arms were pale stalks of cornflowers

And his wrists were fishing line, clear and slack

And his hands were the rescue cats growing fatter and fatter,

and his thumbs were what we never said.

and his handshakes were the wishbone on Thanksgiving day.

and the last time we talked it was famine.


And I was a bedroom with torn sheets and broken blinds.

And his face was black ice, in the curved canyon road,

his addiction and mine.

# BLUE

Blue is for possibility, the fog in the mountains,

The dragonfly's wing, that blue, in the evening light;

The ocean's edge, the blue of redemption;

The blue of the bird, the robin's blue egg;

The effervescent blue of home;

Self-effacing blue, the blue of open sky;

prismatic blue, speaking hopeful truths;

The blue of what always is;

Blue of tributaries, blue of grass;

The blue of flame, the blue of the spring tide;

Turquoise blue, bright strength of stone;

The blue of fish scales, the afternoon shadow, the open compass.

# ABOUT ATMOSPHERE PRESS

Atmosphere Press is an independent, full-service publisher for excellent books in all genres and for all audiences. Learn more about what we do at atmospherepress.com.

We encourage you to check out some of Atmosphere's latest releases, which are available at Amazon.com and via order from your local bookstore:

*In the Cloakroom of Proper Musings,* a lyric narrative by Kristina Moriconi

*Lucid_Malware.zip,* poetry by Dylan Sonderman

*The Unordering of Days,* poetry by Jessica Palmer

*It's Not About You,* poetry by Daniel Casey

*A Dream of Wide Water,* poetry by Sharon Whitehill

*Radical Dances of the Ferocious Kind,* poetry by Tina Tru

*The Woods Hold Us,* poetry by Makani Speier-Brito

*My Cemetery Friends: A Garden of Encounters at Mount Saint Mary in Queens, New York,* nonfiction and poetry by Vincent J. Tomeo

*Report from the Sea of Moisture,* poetry by Stuart Jay Silverman

*The Enemy of Everything,* poetry by Michael Jones

*The Stargazers,* poetry by James McKee

*The Pretend Life,* poetry by Michelle Brooks

*Minnesota and Other Poems,* poetry by Daniel N. Nelson

# ABOUT THE AUTHOR

Kristin Rose Jutras attended Stanford University and received a B.A. in English Literature with a concentration in Creative Writing. After college, she worked in science publishing at Pearson Education and The New York Times Digital, then became involved in microbiology and neurogenetics research at Yale University.

Kristin received her M.F.A. in Fiction and Poetry from Fairfield University. She has experience in freelance journalism, travel writing, and science writing. She taught English Literature at Fairfield University for 4 years, and is now the Director of Communications and Creative Services at the Fralin Life Sciences Institute at Virginia Tech.

Kristin has published her poems and creative non-fiction in *Poems in the Waiting Room*, *Spry Literary Magazine*, the *I'm Possible Project*, and the *Elephant Journal*.

Kristin lives in the blue mountains of Virginia with her husband and their dog, Fee, and poorly behaved puppy, Fred.

www.ingramcontent.com/pod-product-compliance
Lightning Source LLC
Chambersburg PA
CBHW032122050726
47590CB00008B/2928